IMAGES
of America

AROUND
PORTSMOUTH
IN THE VICTORIAN ERA
THE PHOTOGRAPHY OF
THE DAVIS BROTHERS

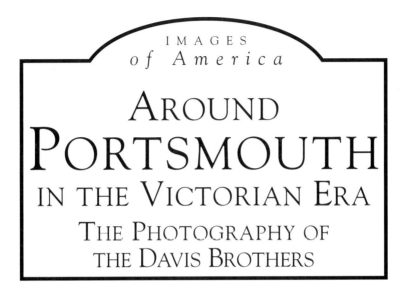

IMAGES
of America

AROUND
PORTSMOUTH
IN THE VICTORIAN ERA
THE PHOTOGRAPHY OF
THE DAVIS BROTHERS

James Dolph and Ronan Donohoe

ARCADIA

First published 1997
Copyright © James Dolph and Ronan Donohoe, 1997

ISBN 0-7524-0281-1

Published by Arcadia Publishing,
an imprint of the Chalford Publishing Corporation,
One Washington Center, Dover, New Hampshire 03820.
Printed in Great Britain

Library of Congress Cataloging-in-Publication Data applied for

Contents

Acknowledgments

A special thanks to the following individuals and institutions for their assistance with this book: Jane Porter, Rodman Philbrick, the Portsmouth Athenaeum, and the Portsmouth Historical Society.

The authors want to thank their families for their forbearing support and encouragement: Bonnie, Miranda, Mallory, and Adam Dolph; and Laura, Charles, and Elizabeth Donohoe.

Introduction

Portsmouth citizens were first exposed to photography on a winter day in 1840. On February 22, the *Portsmouth Journal* announced that Samuel P. Long, a professor of painting at the Portsmouth Academy, had made a photographic image of the Universalist church and its surrounding scenery. Professor Long would have used the photographic process that had been developed only a year earlier by French artist Louis Jacques Daguerre. Whatever happened to Long's early photographs isn't known, but he must have pondered what effect the new art of photography would have on painting. In any case, he opened the doors to a new technological wonder that would capture images of Portsmouth and its surroundings for future generations to enjoy and learn from.

Photography arrived on American shores at quite an auspicious time. Americans were on the move: leaving the East to settle the West; leaving small towns and rural hamlets to seek their fortunes in the nation's emerging metropolitan centers. Photographers would be there to capture and preserve the images of home and loved ones and at greater convenience and less cost than painters. Ensuing decades would witness the departure of sons for Civil War battlefields and the return of others to extravagant celebrations such as Portsmouth's 250th anniversary in 1873. (One suspects the citizens of Portsmouth were attempting to get a jump on the rest of the country by celebrating a 250th three years before the nation would celebrate a mere centennial.)

By the 1850s photographic studios had opened throughout the country and were becoming commonplace. The town of Portsmouth was no exception, with at least two photographic studios in business at any given time. By the close of the century, nearly twenty different photographers had operated studios in Portsmouth at one time or another. One of the most successful of these photographers was Lewis Gilman Davis, who founded the Davis Brothers Photographic Studio. Born in Ripley, Maine, in 1833, Lewis had settled in Portsmouth by 1856 and opened his first studio on Daniel Street. The ambitious young photographer advertised "Pictures for the Millions" priced lower than those of any other artist north of Boston. A year later he entered into a lifelong partnership with his younger brother Charles. In 1859 the brothers expanded the enterprise and opened a second studio in Exeter, New Hampshire. Newspaper advertisements indicate that the younger brother Charles managed the Exeter studio, while Louis was primarily responsible for the Portsmouth business. The Exeter studio was sold to William N. Hobbs in 1866 and thereafter both brothers concentrated their efforts in Portsmouth.

As Davis Brothers continued to prosper and expand, its success became reflected in the brothers' domestic arrangements and civic involvements. Charles and his wife Mattie built a handsome and commodious residence on Miller Avenue, a new neighborhood which at the time was attracting many of the city's successful businessmen. Their only child, Marion Tucker, was for a time associated with the family business. Lewis built an ample residence at the corner of Highland and Broad Streets where he and his wife Cyrena raised four children. The eldest of these, Charles Albert, followed in his father's footsteps and pursued a career in photography but abandoned this first profession and went on to become a prominent geologist. Lewis was for many years active in city politics and organizations such as the New Hampshire Mechanic Association.

By the 1870s, stereoscopic views (double photographs mounted on a single card and viewed through an optical instrument producing a three-dimensional illusion) were becoming very popular, especially with tourists. The Davis brothers took full advantage of this market and sold thousands of stereopticon images of places including Portsmouth, New Castle, Rye, and the Hamptons in New Hampshire; the United States Navy Yard across the Piscataqua River from Portsmouth; Kittery, Kittery Point, and York, Maine; and the Isles of Shoals ten miles offshore from Portsmouth.

Their business was so successful that the studio was expanded and moved several times. In 1889, the brothers bought the business of photographer Oliver H. Cook at 5 Congress Street. Charles ran the new studio while Lewis operated the old studio on Pleasant Street. But by the mid-1890s, time was catching up with the two brothers and the only studio in operation was the one on Congress Street. In 1903 the business was sold to Ralph Boyd. In 1909, Lewis died at the age of seventy-five. Charles died two years later in 1911, also at the age of seventy-five.

Today, a vast collection of Davis Brothers images, depicting the way life used to be in Portsmouth and its surrounding environs, has been preserved by the Portsmouth Athenaeum. This book is a collection of these images, focusing primarily on stereopticon cards.

One
Street Scenes

MARKET STREET. This view looks across Market Square into Market Street. Signs displaying icons such as the mortar and pestle seen on the front of the building on the left are a reminder of an earlier time when literacy could not be assumed.

PLEASANT STREET, 1881.
Seen in the left foreground is the Treadwell House (still standing), known for years as the Elks Home and now the galleries of Northeast Auctions. The house in the center has been demolished; its site has been incorporated into the grounds of the Governor Langdon House. The tall church spire is that of the Universalist church, no longer standing; in front of it is the parsonage of the North Church, which was moved to Sturbridge Village.

CONGRESS STREET, CIRCA 1870. The western end of the street shown here was still a fashionable residential neighborhood at this time. Picket fences, trees, and shrubs west of the Kearsarge House stand in sharp contrast to the commercial character of the street today.

ISLINGTON STREET. Long gone is the streamlined, almost tailored elegance of this stretch of Islington Street from Cornwall Street looking in toward the center of town. The Goodwin House at the far left has been moved to Strawbery Banke Museum. The Trafton House in the center, with its rusticated quoining, remains. The residences beyond it have been demolished for the sake of commercial expansion.

THE SPRUCE CREEK BRIDGE. This old wooden bridge once spanned Spruce Creek and connected Kittery to Kittery Point. The Lady Pepperrell House can be seen amidst the trees on the right.

A PORTSMOUTH MORNING CHRONICLE ADVERTISEMENT, NOVEMBER 4, 1856. This is the first known advertisement to announce Lewis Gilman Davis as a photographer in Portsmouth.

RICHARDS AVENUE, CIRCA 1875. Originally developed in the year 1805, Richards Avenue has undergone numerous name changes. It has been Cow Lane, Joshua Street, and Auburn Street. During the Civil War, the street was beautified by the lining of both sides with elm trees. The planting was done primarily through the efforts of Henry L. Richards and Dr. Robert O. Treadwell. Richards was killed at the Battle of Gettysburg on July 2, 1863, and the street was subsequently named for him. The house on the left was constructed during the War of 1812 and is historically known as the Long-Ladd House.

CONGRESS STREET. Of interest in this image of Congress Street are the two small houses just beyond the North Church in the left foreground. The first of these two remains behind the 1950s facade of the Eagle Photo shop.

THE HENRY SHERBURNE HOUSE. Deer Street in the old North End of Portsmouth is remembered nowadays as an ethnic enclave, formerly home to many of the town's Italian families among others. And so it was when urban renewal dismantled and permanently altered most of the neighborhood in the 1960s. The camera's eye captured these two handsome Deer Street residences occupied by Portsmouth's prosperous merchant class in the 1870s.

MARKET SQUARE, CIRCA 1880. Thacher's Pharmacy is shown here on the ground floor of the Pierce Block at the corner of Market Street. Hatch's jewelry store appears to the left and the Portsmouth Athenaeum beyond. The plaster-like material once applied to the facade above Thacher's has been removed, and the whole presents a more unified appearance today.

A THACHER, DRUGGIST & APOTHECARY ADVERTISEMENT, 1886 PORTSMOUTH CITY DIRECTORY.

THE H. FISHER ELDREDGE ESTATE. H. Fisher Eldredge, Frank Jones's contemporary and competitor in the brewing business built this home and carriage house on spacious grounds on Miller Avenue between 1879 and 1881. The house is now an apartment house and the carriage house was for many years the home of the now defunct YWCA; it has since been remodeled into condominiums.

PLEASANT STREET. This segment of Pleasant Street from State Street to Market Square was known in colonial times as the Parade and was used for training the town's militia.

CONGRESS STREET. This view down Congress Street toward Market Square shows the now-demolished Cutter House on the right. Dr. Ammi Cutter served as a surgeon at the siege of Louisbourg and entertained President James Monroe in this house in 1817.

STATE STREET. The Methodist church on the right was acquired by a Jewish congregation and renamed Temple Israel in 1912. It is apparent from this view looking down State Street toward the Piscataqua River that the steeple that once adorned the building has been removed.

THE SOUTH MILL BRIDGE. The old sawmill on the site of today's Olde Mill Fish Market carries signs that read "Shorts," "Planing," and "Sawing." Except for the introduction of the fish market, the scene at the intersection of Marcy and South Streets remains virtually unchanged to this day.

THE SOUTH MILL POND. This 1890s view, taken from the grassy slope of what is now the municipal complex known as "City Hill," shows the recently constructed causeway spanning the South Mill Pond and providing access by way of Junkins Avenue to the new Cottage Hospital built in 1895. Prominent in the background are the Rockingham House and the spires of the North and Universalist churches.

MIDDLE STREET. Presenting a quite urban, almost metropolitan appearance on Middle Street, the William F. Parrott houses were built in 1864-65 from designs by the prominent Boston architect Gridley J.F. Bryant. Bryant was connected to another of Portsmouth's most citified structures; Frank Jones hired Bryant to enlarge his Rockingham Hotel in 1870.

AN ENOCH J. CONNER ADVERTISEMENT, 1890 *PORTSMOUTH CITY DIRECTORY.*

THE NORTH MILL BRIDGE. This is now part of Maplewood Avenue as it crosses the North Mill Pond. The construction of bridges such as this one effectively cut off navigation to upstream points to all but the smallest craft.

STATE STREET, *CIRCA* 1875.

MARKET SQUARE. This view looks across Market Square and to Daniel Street. Taken *circa* 1880, this photograph shows True Ball's narrow saloon nestled between the two buildings on the right. The building to the left of the saloon is now occupied by Cafe Brioche. Noticeable on the third floor of the building on the far left is the sign identifying the Knights of Pythias Hall.

ALBERT E. RAND,

— DEALER IN —

Choice Family Groceries,

MEATS AND PROVISIONS.

Tobacco,

Cigars and

Confectionery.

PURE CIDER VINEGAR

a Specialty.

NO. 43 MIDDLE STREET,   PORTSMOUTH, N. H.

ALBERT E. RAND ADVERTISEMENT, 1890 PORTSMOUTH CITY DIRECTORY.

Two
Winter Scenes

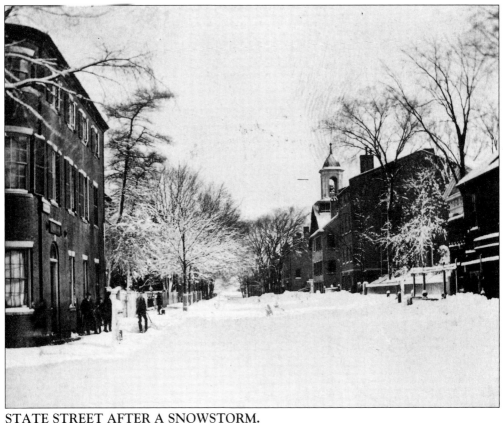

STATE STREET AFTER A SNOWSTORM.

THE GOVERNOR LANGDON HOUSE AFTER THE ICE STORM OF JANUARY 28, 1886.

STATE STREET AFTER THE ICE STORM OF JANUARY 28, 1886.

24

STORM DAMAGE AFTER THE ICE STORM OF JANUARY 28, 1886. Early in the morning the day after the storm, all available city work teams began clearing the streets of limbs fallen because of the weight of the ice. The absence of utility poles and wires simplified their task considerably.

PLEASANT STREET AFTER THE ICE STORM OF JANUARY 28, 1886. An excerpt from the January 29th edition of the *Portsmouth Chronicle* described the great ice storm as follows: "Never within our recollection were the trees throughout the city so completely and heavily coated with ice, from the ground to the tips of the smallest twigs.

AUSTIN STREET.

OXEN ROLLING PORTSMOUTH STREETS. After heavy snowstorms, the streets were "rolled" to compact the snow and provide a good surface for sleighs. In this image of 1858, no less than eight yoke of oxen can be seen working at the intersection of State and Pleasant Streets. Over the second-story windows of the building on the left is the sign identifying the "Daguerrean Gallery" of the Davis brothers.

Photographs.

MR. CHAS. DAVIS, of the firm of DAVIS BRO's would inform the citizens of Exeter and vicinity that he has taken rooms at No. 40, Water St., over the store of John L. Lovering, where he is prepared to execute all kinds of PHOTOGRAPHIC PICTURES, in a manner which cannot be surpassed. Photographs taken of any required size, and colored in oil or water colors. Ambrotypes, Malenatypes and every other invented picture, made and warranted, at fair prices.

Particular attention paid to copying old Daguerreotypes. And to those having pictures of deceased friends, he would say that, you can have a nice large Photograph, suitable for Framing, taken from the smallest Daguerreotype. Also, Particular attention paid to Photographing Residences, &c.

Every variety of Cases and Frames constantly on hand and for sale cheap.

The public are generally invited to call and examine Specimens. Remember the No.

44   40 Water Street, Exeter N H.

AN *EXETER GAZETTE* ADVERTISEMENT, MARCH 14, 1859. Shortly after Lewis opened his business in Portsmouth, he formed a partnership with his brother Charles. Lewis operated the business in Portsmouth while Charles operated a studio in Exeter from 1859 to 1866.

CONGRESS STREET, JANUARY 18, 1867.

THE EXCHANGE BUILDING, PLEASANT STREET, JANUARY 18, 1867.

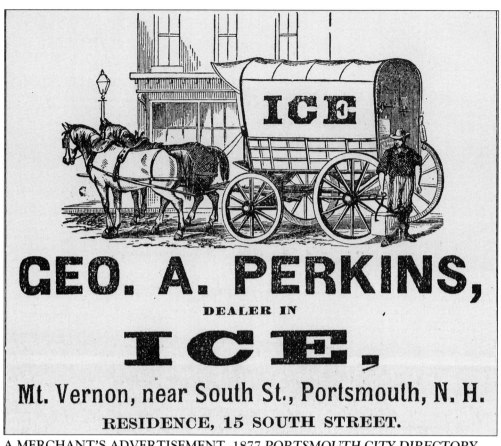

A MERCHANT'S ADVERTISEMENT, 1877 PORTSMOUTH CITY DIRECTORY.

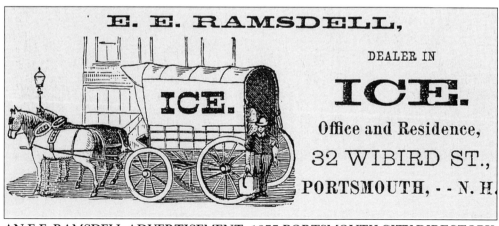

AN E.E. RAMSDELL ADVERTISEMENT, 1877 PORTSMOUTH CITY DIRECTORY.

Three

Return of the
Sons and Daughters
of Portsmouth

THE FIRE ENGINE HOUSE, COURT STREET. A large spruce arch that spanned the width of the building was erected near the sidewalk. It was decorated with the names of the fire engines and a large eagle and shield surrounded by two flags. Flags, wreaths, and a stuffed owl decorated the building itself. Today the building is occupied by Baker & Wright Auto Electric Service.

AN ADVERTISEMENT FOR DAVIS BROTHERS MEMENTOS. Throughout the nineteenth century, as Portsmouth declined as an important seaport, young men and women of the time migrated elsewhere to earn their livelihoods. To bring them home for a visit great celebrations named "Return of the Sons and Daughters of Portsmouth" were held. The largest of these occurred on July 4, 1873, the year of the city's 250th anniversary. The event developed into a four-day celebration that included a mile-long parade, decorated homes and streets, fireworks, boat races, river excursions, banquets, and speeches.

A PRINTING OFFICE, CORNER OF STATE AND PLEASANT STREETS. The block at the corner of State and Pleasant Streets was occupied by two newspapers, the *Journal* and the *Times*, and the shoe manufacturer Thomas S. Nowell. A room in this block was used as general headquarters for various committees organizing the homecoming celebration. Today the building is the home of the State Street Saloon and apartments.

MARKET STREET, LOOKING NORTH. In addition to the storefront decorations, an arch was erected at the intersection of Market and Bow Streets. Notice the provision for crossing muddy streets.

THE WILLIAM R. PRESTON HOUSE. The residence of William R. Preston on Middle Street was decorated with flags and bouquets of flowers. Over the entrance gate hung a huge eagle that may have been carved by famed woodcarver John Bellamy.

THE WILLIAM H.Y. HACKETT HOUSE, CONGRESS STREET. William H.Y. Hackett, an influential attorney and prominent citizen, decorated his home with flags and a banner that read, "We miss one Star." The banner referred to the late Thomas Starr King (1824–1864). Raised in Portsmouth, King is credited with publicizing the beauty of New Hampshire in his book, *The White Hills, Their Legends, Landscapes and Poetry.* The house was moved to Hill Street shortly after the turn of the century. The Portsmouth YMCA was constructed on the site. In later years the YMCA building was to become Goodman's Clothing Store.

THE MAIN TENT. A 300-foot tent was erected on Wibird Hill (the present site of the Edgewood Manor Nursing Home). On the celebration day, thirty-four hundred plates were laid for the honored guests. The menu for the mass meal shows that dinner consisted of cold meats, bread, pastry, and cake with cold water and lemonade. On the evening of the Fourth, several different bands provided a musical background while the assembled crowd socialized and renewed acquaintances. High winds nearly destroyed this tent on the eve of the big event.

THE ROCKINGHAM HOUSE, STATE STREET. The Rockingham House, a commercial hotel, was decorated with flags and streamers wherever they could be tastefully displayed. The structure shown here was nearly destroyed by fire in September 1884. It was enlarged and remodeled under the entrepreneurial guidance of Portsmouth's brewery and railroad magnate, Frank Jones.

THE GOVERNOR ICHABOD GOODWIN HOUSE, ISLINGTON STREET. The Honorable Ichabod Goodwin, governor of New Hampshire from 1859 to 1861, decorated his home with three lines of flags and a welcome banner that extended clear across the street. His porch was also decorated with flags and a pious motto, "Faith, Hope and Charity." The Goodwin House was moved to Strawbery Banke Museum in February 1963. At that time it was under the threat of demolition for commercial expansion.

THE MAIN TENT ENTRANCE. A Roman arch was erected at the main entrance. Its columns were ornamented with American shields and wreaths and capped with flowers. Over the entrance was the word "Welcome" woven in flowers with the United States Coat of Arms above it.

Four
United States Navy Yard

THE SHIPYARD BRIDGE, CIRCA 1880. A bridge connecting the shipyard to the mainland was constructed in 1825 at a cost of $2,373. It was eventually replaced with the railroad and automobile bridge that is now located at the shipyard's main entrance.

THE PORTSMOUTH NAVAL SHIPYARD WATERFRONT, *CIRCA* 1880. This view depicts Shiphouses 4 and 5 as seen from Portsmouth, showing the masting shears, which were used like cranes to raise masts onto ships.

THE DECK OF THE USS *SABINE*. The *Sabine* was used as a training ship at the shipyard from 1872 to 1877.

THE UNITED STATES MARINE BARRACKS, CIRCA 1870. From the year 1806 until 1987, a detachment of US Marines had always been assigned to the shipyard for the protection of the government-owned property. In 1828 a permanent brick barracks was constructed. Local folklore states that military prisoners shackled with ball and chain cleared the land and helped construct the building. In 1977 the building was placed on the National Register of Historic Places.

A BIRD'S-EYE VIEW OF SHIPYARD, AUGUST 12, 1865. According to the *Portsmouth Journal of Literature and Politics*, the Davis brothers visited the shipyard and took numerous stereoscopic views, including one from the cupola on Building 13. This view shows rows of cannons (in what is now known as Gun and Shot Park); to their right is the Ordnance Building (Building 22) and in the foreground are miscellaneous wooden buildings that were hastily constructed during the Civil War.

BACK CHANNEL AND SEAVEY ISLAND. The Portsmouth Naval Shipyard consists of six islands that have been connected together since its establishment in 1800. The largest of the six was named Seavey Island (shown in this *circa* 1870 view); it was purchased by the US Navy in 1866.

BUILDING 22, CIRCA 1870. Building 22 was originally built as the Ordnance Building in 1857. The gun carriages for numerous famed naval vessels of the nineteenth century were constructed in this building. In 1912, under the watchful eye of Chief Boatswain William Lowell Hill, a reading room and bowling alley were established in the building. This was a milestone in establishing a quality of life program for the military personnel assigned to the shipyard. Today the building is used as an Officers' Club with a pizza parlor and barbershop.

BUILDING 22, EAST WING, CIRCA 1870. The east wing of Building 22 served as the boiler plant, providing power and heat to the shipyard.

SHIPHOUSES 4 AND 5. Throughout the last century, over forty naval vessels were constructed at the shipyard, usually inside large, open, barn-like structures called shiphouses. These buildings allowed work to continue when the elements of a New England winter would have rendered it impossible to work outside. Vessels were constructed on shipways that allowed the ships to slide into the river upon completion of their hulls.

BUILDINGS 18 AND 19.
Building 18 (shown in the foreground) was constructed during the Civil War as a machine shop, smithery, and foundry. Today it is used as office space for various engineering departments on the shipyard. Building 19 (shown above on the immediate left) was constructed in the 1850s as the coppersmiths' and watchmen's quarters.

QUARTERS B. Quarters B was constructed in 1849 as a residence for the captain of the shipyard. At that time, the captain of the yard was the second in command and performed the duties of an executive officer under the commanding officer of the shipyard. Today the residence is the home of the production officer and his or her family.

QUARTERS C AND D. Quarters C and D were housed in a two-tenement dwelling built for the lieutenant and surgeon of the shipyard. The structure cost less than $16,000 to build in 1832 and has been used as officers' quarters for shipyard personnel since that time.

OFFICERS' QUARTERS G, H, I, AND J. These quarters were originally constructed in 1828 as a barracks for the ordinary seamen stationed at the facility. The building was deemed suitable to accommodate two hundred men. Shortly after its completion, a draft of one hundred men arrived at the shipyard from the Boston Naval Shipyard to work on the rigging and masting of the sloop of war *Concord*. At Boston, the men lived in cramped style aboard the receiving ship *Independence*. While at this shipyard they were quartered in this barracks, which the men gratefully nicknamed "Sailors' Snug Harbor."

DAVIS BROTHERS,

Ambrotype and Photograph

ARTISTS,

AND DEALERS IN

Oval Gilt, Rosewood, and Black Walnut

FRENCH AND AMERICAN FRAMES,

No. 17 Pleasant Street,

Directly opposite the Post Office,

PORTSMOUTH, N. H.

Large size Photographs, Plain India Ink, and colored in Oil or Water Colors, taken from life, or copied from old pictures, magnified to any size desired, and warranted to give satisfaction. Cartes de Visite in Vignette and all other styles. Ambrotypes taken and every kind of Photographic work done in the best style of the art.

A DAVIS BROTHERS ADVERTISEMENT, 1864 PORTSMOUTH CITY DIRECTORY.

QUARTERS A, RESIDENCE OF THE SHIPYARD COMMANDANT. This home was constructed during the War of 1812 by John Locke of Portsmouth for the sum of $3,500. The oldest building on the facility, it is still in use as the residence for the shipyard commander.

THE USS *AGAMENTICUS*, AUGUST 12, 1865. Constructed during the Civil War, the *Agamenticus* was the first of three double-turreted ironclad monitors constructed at the Portsmouth Naval Shipyard. It was commissioned on May 5, 1865, in anticipation of doing battle with the Confederate ironclad ram *Stonewall* that was reported to be crossing from Europe. Nothing ever came of this and the vessel operated between Maine and Massachusetts until 1869 when it was renamed *Terror*. In 1870 it was assigned to the North Atlantic Fleet, operating primarily between Key West, Florida, and Havana, Cuba. The vessel was decommissioned in 1872 and broken up in 1874.

Five
Churches

THE CHURCH ON THE COMMON IN GREENLAND, NH. This church, built in 1756, was remodeled in 1834 and once again in 1881. The elegance of the earlier nineteenth-century design can be seen in this photograph, taken in 1877.

THE UNIVERSALIST CHURCH. This wooden church stood on Pleasant Street opposite the Governor Langdon House. It was erected in 1808, burned in 1896, and was replaced by a brick edifice which itself burned in 1947. The site has since been the parking lot for a supermarket and more recently a succession of banks.

THE INTERIOR OF THE UNIVERSALIST CHURCH. This view shows the *trompe l'oeil* decoration of the sanctuary, reflecting a popular style of the nineteenth century.

ST. JOHN'S CHURCH. St. John's Episcopal Church was completed in 1807, replacing an earlier Queen's Chapel which, renamed St. John's after the Revolution, was destroyed by fire in 1806. The church's bell, captured from the French at Louisbourg in 1745, survived the fire and was recast by Paul Revere in 1807. Many of Portsmouth's pre-Revolutionary elite are interred in the adjacent tombs and burial ground.

THE NORTH CHURCH. This brick structure, built in Market Square in 1854, replaced an earlier wooden Congregational church. The steeple and window trimming, now painted white, originally appeared in the earth tones deemed more attractive to mid-nineteenth-century taste.

THE NORTH CHURCH INTERIOR. The North Church (Congregational) is decorated for the celebration of its bicentennial on July 19, 1871. The wheel in the center displays the names of former pastors and the dates of their pastorates.

THE SOUTH CHURCH. The South Church was built between 1824 and 1826. There has always been some controversy as to whether the short, square tower adds to or detracts from the Greek Revival lines of this large granite structure. It is now home to the Unitarian-Universalist congregation.

THE SOUTH CHURCH INTERIOR. This is an example of the Victorian taste for decorating interiors with heaps of flowers. The particular church and the occasion cannot be identified. There appears to be an effigy of an early pastor in the center.

CHRISTMAS AT THE SOUTH CHURCH. This early 1870s view shows the church decorated for the Christmas season. The curved pews shown here were replaced at a later date.

CHRIST CHURCH. Workers from the north of England were recruited by Portsmouth brewers and that influx of Englishmen into the expanding western part of town prompted the construction of this second Episcopal church on Madison Street in 1881. This handsome fieldstone structure was tragically destroyed by fire in 1963.

THE FIRST CHRISTIAN CHURCH, CIRCA 1880. Churches of this denomination occupied several different Portsmouth sites. City directories of the 1880s give a Court Street address for this one.

THE BAPTIST CHURCH. Portsmouth has been home to several Baptist congregations. This group organized in 1826 and in 1828 built a church at the west side of the intersection of State and Middle. That edifice was replaced in 1856 with the church pictured here. It was demolished in 1953 and the site is now occupied by a gas station.

Six
Isles of Shoals

THE OCEANIC HOTEL, STAR ISLAND. In the foreground is one of the two-masted, double-ended craft known as "Isles of Shoals boats" that were commonly used by summer visitors for a day on the water.

MISS UNDERHILL'S CHAIR, STAR ISLAND, CIRCA 1870. A group looks over the site of Miss Underhill's chair, marked by the cross. Miss Underhill was a schoolteacher at the Isles of Shoals. She had a favorite spot on the cliff to which she often retreated to read and enjoy the view. On September 11, 1848, the unfortunate Miss Underhill was swept away by a rogue wave that crested the rocks.

THE CAVE AT STAR ISLAND. The Davis brothers' stereoscopic views made this and other images of the rocky shoals startlingly three-dimensional. The visitor perched on these rocks may well have been one who responded to the claim that the Isles of Shoals were ideal for those with respiratory ailments because the islands were "pollen-free."

A *PORTSMOUTH DAILY CHRONICLE* ADVERTISEMENT. By the 1870s a wide variety of stereoscopic views of Portsmouth and vicinity were being offered by Davis Brothers.

APPLEDORE ISLAND. The Laighton family, operators of the Appledore House, invented imaginative and romantic names for various bits of the rocky island landscape. This stark chasm on Appledore was dubbed "Neptune's Hall."

THE STONE CHURCH ON STAR ISLAND. The wooden tower of this simple and lovely church was later replaced with one of stone. Built on the highest spot on the island, the church was listed in guides for mariners as an aid to navigation before a lighthouse was erected and lit on nearby White Island in 1821.

THE WHITE ISLAND LIGHTHOUSE, CIRCA 1865. As with all lighthouses along the coast, this one had been mechanized by the 1980s.

THE GOSPORT HOUSE, STAR ISLAND. Small boarding houses like this provided room and board for those in search of a Star Island holiday before the far grander Oceanic Hotel was built to compete with the Appledore Hotel on nearby Appledore Island.

THE HONTVET HOUSE, SMUTTYNOSE ISLAND. This was the site of the notorious 1873 ax murders of two Norwegian women. German immigrant Louis Wagner was later convicted and hanged for the crime, although doubts about his guilt persist to this day.

THE SMITH MONUMENT, STAR ISLAND. This still-standing monument commemorates the English Captain John Smith, mariner, cartographer, and erstwhile heartthrob of Pocahontas, who first mapped the Isles of Shoals in 1614.

THE APPLEDORE HOUSE. Widely recognized as a gathering place for nineteenth-century literary and artistic figures, the hotel was operated by the Laighton family. In a nearby cottage, the poet Celia Laighton Thaxter turned her parlor into a *salon* which she adorned daily with flowers from her famous Island Garden. The roster of her visitors includes many of the greats of New England's intellectual and artistic circles.

THE LANDING ON APPLEDORE ISLAND. Perhaps waiting to embark on the voyage home, these visitors are dressed to the nines, with no skin exposed and parasols to boot. No need for greasy sunblocks in this crowd.

A SHOALS STEAMER. This is one of the steamers that transported visitors to the Isles of Shoals during the nineteenth century.

Seven
Hotels

THE BOARS HEAD HOTEL, HAMPTON BEACH, NH. Stebbins H. Dumas rose from bellhop at Concord's Phoenix Hotel in 1846 to proprietor of the capitol's Eagle House in 1856; in 1865 he purchased the Boars Head Hotel.

THE GAZEBO AT BOARS HEAD. This gazebo or summer house was built on the headland at the Boars Head Hotel to enhance the grounds and allow even those staying in the less expensive, inland-facing rooms the opportunity to enjoy the panoramic views from Cape Ann to Portsmouth.

THE BOARS HEAD HOTEL, HAMPTON BEACH, NH. S.H. Dumas, proprietor of the Boars Hotel at Hampton Beach, earned the title of colonel by providing the banquets following a gubernatorial inauguration. He is said to have salted the hotel register with the names of Abraham Lincoln, Mrs. John Jacob Astor, and others to up the social cachet of the establishment.

HOTEL,

ＨＡＭＰＴＯＮ ＢＥＡＣＨ, Ｎ. Ｈ.

S. H. DUMAS, PROPRIETOR.

OAR'S HEAD is an abrupt eminence extending into the sea, and forming the dividing point
reen the grand North and South Beaches at Hampton. On the crown of the promontory
Hotel is built. It is so elevated as to command, from window and piazza, a wide view of
sea, Isles of Shoals, and the coast from Cape Ann to Portsmouth. The rooms are well
ted and ventilated, and easily accessible. Every convenience has been provided. A Tele-
h Office, Post Office, Billiard Hall, and Bowling Alley, are connected with the House. It
n miles from Exeter, ten from Newburyport, twelve from Portsmouth, five from Rye
ch, and forty-four from Boston. Five trains pass each way day daily on the Eastern Rail-
l, making close connections with all adjoining roads. Guests leave the Cars at Hampton
ion, three miles from Boar's Head, where coaches will be in readiness.

A BOARS HEAD HOTEL ADVERTISEMENT. This advertisement was printed on the
back of the Davis Brothers stereopticon views of the hotel. The cards must have been very
popular with the tourists vacationing at the Hampton Beach hotel.

THE SAGAMORE HOUSE, RYE, NH.
On March 25, 1865, the *Portsmouth Chronicle* reported that "James Pierce, Esq., who for the past twelve years has been employed on the Vanderbilt Panama Steamers, has purchased the Sagamore House and farm which he purposes to throw open to the public this coming season as a summer resort." Fire broke out in the kitchen as the hotel was being prepared for the summer of 1872. The flames were almost extinguished when a well-meaning person broke a window in the cupola, venting the flames and dooming the elegant hostelry.

THE OCEAN HOUSE AT RYE BEACH, NH.
This hotel boasted an observatory said to seat fifty, featuring views that were reputed to be unexcelled. As was the case with so many of the seacoast hotels of the last century, the Ocean House came to a fiery end in April of 1873.

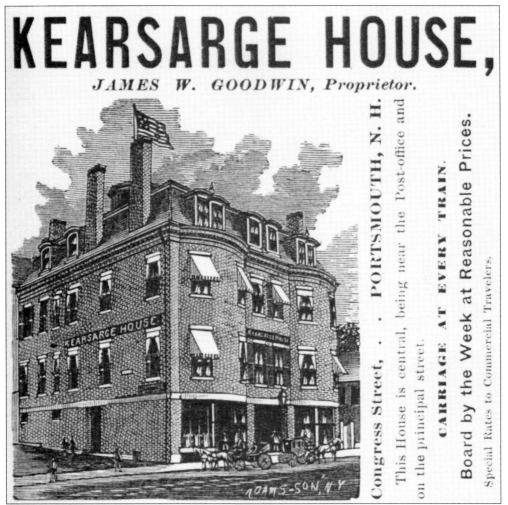

KEARSARGE HOUSE,

JAMES W. GOODWIN, Proprietor.

Congress Street, . . PORTSMOUTH, N. H.

This House is central, being near the Post-office and on the principal street.

CARRIAGE AT EVERY TRAIN.

Board by the Week at Reasonable Prices.

Special Rates to Commercial Travelers.

A KEARSARGE HOUSE ADVERTISEMENT, 1883 *PORTSMOUTH CITY DIRECTORY.*

THE KEARSARGE HOUSE. Named shortly after construction for the Portsmouth-built naval vessel that achieved fame in the Civil War, this building marked the western boundary of Portsmouth's commercial district. Built as a double tenement in the Bulfinch style, it was used almost from the start as a hotel.

DAVIS BROTHERS,
AMBROTYPE & PHOTOGRAPH
ARTISTS,
No. 17 PLEASANT ST. PORTSMOUTH.

CARTES DE VISITES

MADE in every variety of style and as well finished in every respect as any made in this country.— Please examine and compare specimens.

PHOTOGRAPHS

of every style and size—Plain, or worked in India Ink or in Oil or Water colors; also copied any size and finished any style, from every kind of old pictures.

AMBROTYPES

of every size and price. An elegant and very large variety of CASES, comprising every pattern to be found in the market—all of which will be sold with or without pictures, as low as elsewhere.

PICTURE FRAMES,

Comprising every desirable style of Oval Frames to be found in the Boston and New York markets—all of which are for sale cheap for cash. We buy large quantities for cash, and can and will sell cheap.

PHOTOGRAPHIC ALBUMS.

We have a good assortment of these at very low prices. Call and examine before buying elsewhere.

Paper Borders for Pictures; Passapartout little Frames, in great variety, &c. &c. for sale.

Also, all kinds of PHOTOGRAPHIC CHEMICALS.

DAVIS BROTHERS,
17 Pleasant Street, Portsmouth, N. H.
June 28.

A PORTSMOUTH JOURNAL OF LITERATURE AND POLITICS ADVERTISEMENT, JUNE 28, 1862. The Davis brothers flourished and were fast becoming the city's leading photographers (known as photographic artists during their time), as well as purveyors of photographic supplies.

THE SEA COTTAGE AT YORK BEACH, ME. This hotel opened in 1871 and bragged of "a good sea view from three sides of the house." It was later renamed the Hotel Mitchell and still later it was known as the Anchorage Hotel. It was razed to make way for the present Anchorage Motel.

THE ROCKINGHAM HOTEL. Located on State Street, it was once one of the finest hotels north of Boston. This view was taken in 1874. Ten years later the hotel was nearly destroyed by fire. It was rebuilt under the watchful eye of its owner, brewery and railroad tycoon Frank Jones. It continued to receive the traveling public until 1973 when it was converted into condominiums.

THE PEPPERRELL HOTEL, KITTERY POINT, ME. The spacious piazzas of the hotel welcome the carriage trade. Kittery Point boasted several large and fashionable resort hotels of this kind.

A PEPPERRELL HOTEL ADVERTISEMENT, 1890 PORTSMOUTH CITY DIRECTORY.

THE SAGAMORE HOUSE, FROST POINT, RYE, NH. The Sagamore House resort hotel was located at Frost Point, opposite the Wentworth Hotel. The gaff-rigged sloops transported hotel guests as well as local fishermen. The hotel was destroyed by fire in 1871.

THE WASHINGTON HOUSE, RYE BEACH, NH. Shown with its attached barn and stables, the Washington House appears to have been more of a simple summer boarding house than a pretentious seasonal resort.

THE OCEAN HOUSE. This view of the grounds and the broad expanse of the oceanside facade is evidence of the premium placed on "rooms with a view."

THE WENTWORTH HOTEL, NEW CASTLE, NH. This was the *grande dame* of the
seacoast's summer resort hotels. On a clear day the towers were visible from the Isles of Shoals.
The grounds appear stark and treeless to today's eyes; modern viewers are accustomed to seeing
the mature trees that were only saplings when this view was taken.

TENTING ON A BEACH. Not all chose or could afford extended stays in the era's grand hotels. This view of a family campsite suggests an alternative.

ANOTHER TENTING SCENE. These tents are pitched at the edge of a beach. (The photograph is not dated.) Tenting was an option that must have come readily to the minds of Civil War veterans.

THE SEA VIEW HOUSE, RYE BEACH, NH. The elaborate porches shown here on the facade were a great attraction at this hotel, said at the time to compete with the finest at Saratoga.

Eight

Houses and Public Buildings

THE PORTSMOUTH CUSTOMHOUSE, CIRCA 1865. The customhouse was constructed on the corner of State and Pleasant Streets between 1857 and 1860. A new post office was located on the first floor, customs offices and judicial chambers were on the second, and a courtroom was on the third floor. The building passed into private ownership when the new federal building was erected on Daniel Street in 1966.

THE PORTSMOUTH ATHENAEUM. This "Jewel of Market Square" was built after a fire destroyed much of the downtown in 1802. Originally owned by the New Hampshire Fire and Marine Insurance Company, the building has been home to the Portsmouth Athenaeum, a membership library, since 1823. The boards around the trees at the front protected the trees and served as convenient places to post notices.

THE NATHANIEL HAVEN HOUSE. Once they are gone, it is sometimes very difficult to imagine the presence of vanished Federal-style houses like this one. The site of the lost Haven House on High Street is now dominated by the multi-level parking garage and parking lots. By the time this house was destroyed by fire in the 1980s, it had become a somewhat shabby apartment house with a large rear addition.

THE FIRST OFFICE OF *THE NEW HAMPSHIRE GAZETTE*. This is where Daniel Fowle set up New Hampshire's first printing press in 1756. It stood at the junction of Washington and Pleasant Streets.

A NEW HAMPSHIRE GAZETTE ADVERTISEMENT, 1873 *PORTSMOUTH CITY DIRECTORY.*

THE BENJAMIN WEBSTER HOUSE. Benjamin Webster, one of Portsmouth's premier builders of the last century, gave full rein to his architectural abilities and preferences when he erected this stately mansion for himself at the top of Broad Street in 1880. The house survives as the Buckminster Funeral Chapel.

BENJAMIN F. WEBSTER. This 1889 Davis Brothers portrait depicts Benjamin F. Webster.

MAPLEWOOD FARM. Frank Jones, Portsmouth's beer baron, purchased this property at the intersection of Maplewood and Woodbury Avenues in 1867. In 1880, Jones had the original farmhouse greatly enlarged and remolded. Most notable in addition to the house itself were the extensive barns and stables for prize horses and cattle. The grounds were elaborately landscaped with Victorian flowerbeds and greenhouses.

GLEN COTTAGE. This charming residence in the Gothic cottage style made popular in the early nineteenth century by the architect Andrew Jackson Downing once provided contrast to the simpler lines of its neighbors at the corner of Miller and Middle Streets. It was demolished to make room for the late Victorian mansion of former governor James Bartlett, which was in turn demolished to make room for a parking lot.

THE GLOUCESTER HOUSE. The Gloucester House was located on the corner of State and Water (now Marcy) Streets. Once a hotel and boarding house in a neighborhood that became a notorious red-light district, it was among the buildings demolished prior to 1923 to make way for the Memorial Bridge and its approaches.

THE RESIDENCE OF PHOTOGRAPHER CHARLES DAVIS. This still-standing house on Miller Avenue indicates the prosperity that could be achieved by a popular photographer in the Victorian era. In 1883 Charles Davis and his brother and partner Lewis shared a house on Austin Street. By 1886 Charles had taken up residence on Miller Avenue while Lewis had moved to a nearby address at the corner of Highland and Broad Streets.

THE WENTWORTH-GARDNER HOUSE. This image depicts the Wentworth-Gardner House in the 1880s, showing the bank of the Piscataqua River before the present retaining wall was built. This magnificent Georgian mansion on Mechanic Street was built *circa* 1760 as a wedding gift for Thomas Wentworth from his mother, Madame Mark Hunking Wentworth. It was owned for a time by the Metropolitan Museum, which had plans to move it intact to New York and incorporate it into the museum's American Wing.

THE JOHN HART HOUSE. To the right of the Fernald House stood this three-story Federal house, built in 1790, featuring an 1840s colonnade porch and cast-iron railing. It served for a period as a home for aged women, was moved during urban renewal across the street, and now stands as part of "The Hill" (a complex of structures that was moved in the interest of preservation).

A HOUSE ON MILLER AVENUE. Tree-lined Miller Avenue was not always so, as this view of a newly constructed residence will attest.

THE OLD JAIL ON ISLINGTON STREET. This house, on Islington Street at the foot of Summer Street, served as the town's jail from 1782 until 1891, when a new jail was built on Penhallow Street. A stone addition of the 1830s was demolished in 1895; the granite and brick were acquired by the Margeson brothers and used in their Vaughan Street furniture store, which is now Cabot House. The south wall of Cabot House is now well-known as the "Whaling Wall" because of the colorful mural painted on it.

A MERCHANT'S LABEL. The more popular Davis Brothers photographs, in addition to being sold from the studio, were also sold by local merchants to townspeople and tourists. When doing so, the merchants usually affixed their label to the back of the images.

CONGRESS STREET. The camera seems to have captured local citizens setting about their daily chores.

DAVIS BROTHERS,

Ambrotype & Photograph

ARTISTS,

AND DEALERS IN

Oval Gilt, Rosewood, and Black Walnut

FRENCH & AMERICAN FRAMES,

No. 17 Pleasant Street,

Directly opposite the Post Office.

PORTSMOUTH, N. H.

PORCELAIN PICTURES

A FULL-PAGE ADVERTISEMENT, 1867 *PORTSMOUTH CITY DIRECTORY.*

AN INTERIOR VIEW OF THE PORTSMOUTH POST OFFICE, CIRCA 1870. This striking image of the interior of the post office was taken a few years after its construction. The fixtures and fittings might seem a bit grand for a city the size of Portsmouth.

THE CUSTOMHOUSE, CIRCA 1870.

Nine

Fortifications and Lighthouses

PARROTT GUNS AT FORT CONSTITIUTION, *CIRCA* 1880. These guns were mounted on center-pintle iron barbette carriages.

THE RUINS OF A MARTELLO TOWER, NEW CASTLE, NH. The name "Martello" refers to Mortello, Corsica, where these round coastal defensive works were common. Martello towers were constructed along the coasts of the U.S. and Canada in the early nineteenth century. This one was built during the War of 1812 and allowed to fall into disrepair. The ruins remain on the grounds of the United States Coast Guard Station.

FORT CONSTITUTION, NEW CASTLE, NH. The portcullis gate at Fort Constitution imparts an almost medieval appearance. The gate is a part of the 1808 walls, which were built when Jefferson was in office and Congress feared imminent war with Britain. Fort Constitution, earlier known as Fort William and Mary, is now maintained by the NH Parks Department.

THE BLOCK HOUSE AT FORT McCLARY, KITTERY POINT, ME, CIRCA 1880.

THE PORTSMOUTH HARBOR LIGHTHOUSE, CIRCA 1860. This octagonal tower was constructed shortly after the turn of the last century and replaced Portsmouth Harbor's first lighthouse that was built in 1771. It was located where the present lighthouse is at the United States Coast Guard Station in New Castle, NH. The lighthouse, constructed by Benjamin Clark Gilman, was erected on a stone foundation and rose to a height of 85 feet. This image was taken in 1860 after the structure had been shortened.

THE PORTSMOUTH HARBOR LIGHTHOUSE. In 1877 the lighthouse was replaced by the iron structure seen here that is still in service.

THE NUBBLE LIGHTHOUSE IN YORK, ME, *CIRCA* 1890. This is one of a set of twenty stereopticon cards that were taken of York Beach and vicinity in the 1880s. They were immensely popular with the tourists of the day. With the aid of a stereopticon viewer, visitors could recapture in three dimensions the delights of their summer sojourns.

No 86.

Total Sept 1st 1881.

S EREOSCOPIC VIEWS

OF

York Beach and Vicinity,

PUBLISHED BY

DAV'S BROTHERS, PORTSMOUTH, N H.

———•———

No. 1.—Marshall House.— 2 Views.

" 2.—York Harbor from Marshall House.

Nos. 3 and 4.— Views from Marshall House Piazza.

No. 5.—Short Sands.

" 6.—Looking up York River.

" 7.—Roaring Rock.

Nos. 8 and 9.—Views of York Village.

No. 10.—Old Jail — York Village.

" 11.—Hotel Bartlett — Long Beach.

" 12.—Sea Cottage — Long Beach.

" 13.—Nubble.

" 14.—Union Bluff.

" 15.—Union Bluff Hotel.

" 16.—Fairmount Hotel.

" 17.—Fairmount and Union Bluff Hotels.

" 18.—Thompson House.

" 19.—Concordville.

" 20.—Bald Head Cliff — 4 Views.

YORK BEACH, MAINE, AND VICINITY. In the 1880s, Davis Brothers produced a set of twenty stereoscopic views of York Beach and vicinity. The complete list of views shown here was printed on the reverse side of each stereoscopic card.

FORT CONSTITUTION, NEW CASTLE, NH. Granite workers are shown here at the fort sometime during the Civil War.

FORT McCLARY IN KITTERY POINT, ME. Granite workers also were busy at the fort on the other side of the Piscataqua River. The fortifications of the Civil War era were never completed because changing technologies had rendered them obsolete.

Ten
Cemeteries

A ROAD IN THE SOUTH STREET CEMETERY. The cemetery is composed of four sections. That closest to South Street, pictured here, is named Proprietors Cemetery. The Cotton Burial Ground adjoins Proprietors. The middle section is Harmony Grove. The newest (southern) section is the Sagamore Cemetery.

WILLIAM PEPPERRELL'S TOMB IN KITTERY POINT, ME. Located on a mound across from Frisbee's Store in Kittery Point, Maine, the tomb of William Pepperrell and his son Sir William Pepperrell, hero of the Siege of Louisbourg, is shown here decorated, presumably to commemorate the anniversary of a death.

A FLETCHER & TANTON ADVERTISEMENT, 1886 PORTSMOUTH CITY DIRECTORY.

A COBB & CALL
ADVERTISEMENT,
1879
PORTSMOUTH
CITY DIRECTORY.

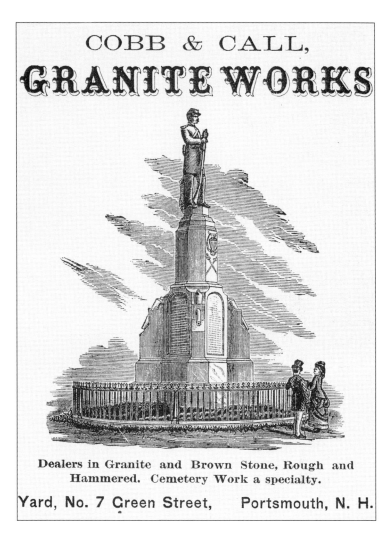

COBB & CALL,
GRANITE WORKS

Dealers in Granite and Brown Stone, Rough and Hammered. Cemetery Work a specialty.

Yard, No. 7 Green Street,   Portsmouth, N. H.

SILAS PHILBRICK & CO.,
— MANUFACTURERS OF —
MARBLE MONUMENTS,
HEAD STONES,
Table Tops, Mantel Pieces, Brown Stone, Soap Stone, and Granite for all purposes.

No. 2 Water St., Portsmouth, N. H.

A SILAS PHILBRICK & CO. ADVERTISEMENT, 1883 PORTSMOUTH CITY DIRECTORY.

A MEMORIAL AT HARMONY GROVE CEMETERY. This massive monument with accompanying urn and plants sits atop a rise in Harmony Grove Cemetery where grieving friends and family of Captain George W. Towle might be consoled and their spirits lifted by the view.

A ROADWAY IN HARMONY GROVE CEMETERY. The landscaping in Harmony Grove was done in a garden style perhaps influenced by the Mount Auburn Cemetery in Cambridge, Massachusetts. The ornamental trees and shrubs appealed to the sentimentality of the era. Stairways and railings delineate family plots.

THE SOUTH STREET CEMETERY. The vantage point of this view is from South Street before turn-of-the-century residential expansion, looking toward the cemetery and the harbor beyond.

Eleven

Waterfront

THE PORTSMOUTH WATERFRONT FROM NOBLES ISLAND, CIRCA 1880.

THE PORTSMOUTH WATERFRONT, CIRCA 1870.

IF YOU DONT CATCH HIM IN 10 DAYS RETURN

ELVIN NEWTON & CO.,

Wholesale Dealers in all kinds of

Salt Water Fish and Lobsters.

STEAK COD A SPECIALTY.

PURE COD LIVER OIL.

COMMERCIAL WHARF, PORTSMOUTH, N.H.

AN ELVIN NEWTON & CO. ADVERTISEMENT, 1886 PORTSMOUTH CITY DIRECTORY.

WINTER ON THE WATERFRONT. This unidentified steam vessel is shown iced over at Walker's Coal Wharf, which stood in the vicinity of the Pier II Restaurant.

GREELY RELIEF EXPEDITION VESSELS MOORED IN PORTSMOUTH HARBOR, AUGUST 8, 1884. A procession of vessels including the USS *Alliance*, *Bear*, *Thetis*, and *Alert* entered Portsmouth Harbor on Friday, August 1, 1884. On board the *Thetis* were the Greely Arctic Expedition survivors. Their journey began in 1881 when thirty men under the command of Lieutenant Aldolphus Greely were sent to Lady Franklin Bay in the Arctic region. They were to set up and man a scientific observation station. Disaster struck when attempts to resupply the expedition in 1882 and 1883 failed. When the men were finally rescued in 1884, only seven had survived. They were brought to the Portsmouth Naval Shipyard for a short stay before traveling on to New York. Lieutenant Greely, a native of Newburyport, remained at the shipyard to recuperate.

THE PORTSMOUTH WATERFRONT, CIRCA 1870.

A GEO. T. VAUGHAN & CO. ADVERTISEMENT, 1886 PORTSMOUTH CITY DIRECTORY.

THE PORTSMOUTH WATERFRONT. This view of the waterfront taken from Ceres Street shows the broad expanse of the Piscataqua from the navy yard in Kittery to the warehouses on Bow Street. The area remains much the same today, with the notable exception of the many buildings which stood between the rear of St. John's Church and the water's edge. The Memorial Bridge now spans the river from a point near where the three-masted ship is tied up.

THE NEW CASTLE, NH, WATERFRONT. This early waterfront view of New Castle includes an interesting glimpse of a crude gundalow in the foreground.

Twelve
Historic House Museums

THE JACKSON HOUSE. The Jackson House on Northwest Street in the Christian Shore part of town is certainly one of the region's most ancient relics. Built on land that sloped to the water's edge in the 1660s, the structure's extremely picturesque roofline over the back ell (or lean-to) is not original, but rather was added during the eighteenth century. Richard Jackson built the house and generations of Jacksons lived in it until the house was sold to S.P.N.E.A. (The Society for the Preservation of New England Antiquities) in the 1920s.

THE MAC PHEADRIS-WARNER HOUSE, CIRCA 1880. Built for Archibald MacPheadris in 1715 and long considered to be one of the finest of its kind in the region, this house was rented from 1742 to 1759 by Royal Governor Benning Wentworth. The house passed from the Sherburne family to the Warner House Association in 1931 to prevent the house being demolished to make way for a gasoline station.

THE STAIR HALLWAY, MAC PHEADRIS-WARNER HOUSE.

THE PARLOR OF THE MAC PHEADRIS-WARNER HOUSE.

SPARHAWK HALL AT KITTERY POINT, ME. This baronial seat was built by Sir William Pepperrell in 1742 as a wedding present for his daughter Elizabeth and her husband, Nathaniel Sparhawk. The site was to the rear of the Kittery Point Congregational Church at the end of Sparhawk Lane. Before the house was razed in the 1960s, some of the interiors were dismantled and reinstalled elsewhere.

THE WENTWORTH-COOLIDGE MANSION. This was the home of Royal Governor Benning Wentworth and, in the late nineteenth century, the summer home of Boston investor and society leader John Templeman Coolidge III. The number of stereopticon cards devoted to the house and its historic furnishings demonstrates the long-standing public interest in historic houses as tourist destinations.

THE CARRIAGEWAY LEADING TO THE WENTWORTH-COOLIDGE MANSION.

THE COUNCIL CHAMBER OF THE WENTWORTH-COOLIDGE MANSION. The elaborately carved chimney piece in the Council Room of the Wentworth-Coolidge Mansion was locally made from an English pattern book. The design chosen by the royal governor is also found in the countryseat of Wentworth's contemporary, Sir Robert Walpole, the first prime minister of Great Britain.

ANOTHER VIEW OF THE COUNCIL CHAMBER. The portraits in this 1870s image are of various Wentworth relatives and ancestors.

THE PARLOR OVERLOOKING THE COUNCIL CHAMBER. The flocked wallpaper of Governor Wentworth's day is still in place, but the oriental rugs preferred in the last century are gone in the name of today's curatorial accuracy.

THE GOVERNOR LANGDON HOUSE. Always a standout, this house was pronounced by President Washington on his visit in 1791 to be "one of the few good houses in town." The handsome mansion shown here is much as it appears today except for the nineteenth-century stone railings, iron gates, wooden trellises, and the essential mounting block at the curb.

Thirteen
Schools

PORTSMOUTH HIGH SCHOOL. Getting a head start on the holidays is not altogether a new thing, as evidenced by this picture of Portsmouth High School scholars assembled for a holiday program on December 9, 1878. The building on Daniel Street, now a realty office, is shown festooned with doubtlessly very inflammable garlands; the walls are adorned with the sentiments of the Christmas season. The decor appears far more cheerful than do the scholars.

PORTSMOUTH ACADEMY, OCTOBER 1881. The academy was constructed in 1806 to provide college preparatory training for the children of Portsmouth's more fortunate families. In 1895 the structure became home to the Portsmouth Public Library.

THE FRANKLIN SCHOOL. This unpretentious brick schoolhouse was built on Maplewood Avenue in 1847. Once popularly known as the Christian Shore School, the building has been converted into apartments.

Fourteen
Industry

THE PORTSMOUTH STEAM FACTORY, CIRCA 1870. The Portsmouth Steam Factory, constructed in the 1840s, was located on Hill Street opposite Pearl Street. The factory employed nearly four hundred individuals in the manufacture of cotton fabrics. In 1866 it was reorganized as the Kearsarge Mills and in 1880 a disastrous fire nearly destroyed the building. In the 1890s it was converted into the Portsmouth Machine Company with an iron foundry. Today the building is occupied by JSA Architects and a publishing company.

THE PORTSMOUTH RAILROAD STATION, CIRCA 1865. The Eastern Railroad first reached Portsmouth in 1840, but the station shown here near the intersection of Bridge and Deer Streets was not built until 1863. The arrival of the railroad meant a significant shift in business activity from the waterfront to this neighborhood. The station is no longer standing.

THE PORTSMOUTH SHOE COMPANY, ISLINGTON STREET, *CIRCA* 1890. The Portsmouth Shoe Company was organized in 1886 and manufactured ladies' boots and shoes. There were twelve hundred workers employed in the factory in 1896. The building was demolished sometime before World War II.

LOOKING ACROSS NORTH MILL POND, CIRCA 1870. This view from Clinton Street shows the fortress-like roundhouse used for the repair of railway locomotives on the far shore. Remnants of the structure can be seen along the water's edge today.

Fifteen
Miscellany

A BARN INTERIOR, CIRCA 1880. Such was the farmer's reward for a season of hard labor.

WARREN AND NAN TOBEY.
Before there were Brownie cameras, studio shots of children dressed in their Sunday best were considered essential family records.

A FLORAL ARRANGEMENT.
This undated floral arrangement was likely one of the many photographed by the Davis brothers at funeral parlors.

A VIEW OF PORTSMOUTH FROM LINCOLN HILL.

A SUNDAY GATHERING, *CIRCA* 1880.

Portsmo. February 12th 1776

Dear & honoured Papa

Doctor Brackett has just desired me to write you — he says if you will bring me home, a watch, laced Hat Sword & Pistols — I have endeavored to be a good boy ever since you have been gone have attended School, & minded my Book my dear Mamma, & brother & Sisters are well I have a fine little Sister since you have been gone — I want to see you much, & hope it wont be long before I shall have that pleasure — it will afford the greatest happiness to your most dutifull son

Henry Sherburn Langdon

Woodbury Langdon, Esq.

A LETTER WRITTEN BY HENRY LANGDON TO HIS FATHER WOODBURY LANGDON, FEBRUARY 12, 1776. The original letter was photographed sometime around 1880. Another use for the photographer's art was to reproduce and thus preserve for posterity documents like this, which capture the childish intimacies of a family's past. The 1776 date was of no small significance a hundred years after the start of the Revolution.

THE SHANTYVILLE IN KITTERY, ME. The words "Shantyville, Kittery" are handwritten on the reverse of this undated image.

THE ROLLINS HOMESTEAD, NEWINGTON, NH. The Rollins Homestead is shown as it appeared in the late nineteenth century.

THE TOWN PARADE IN GREENLAND, NH. By the last quarter of the nineteenth century, some Portsmouth families regarded Greenland as a desirable country retreat. Mature elms are in the background in this 1877 photograph, while wooden guards protect the young trees in the foreground.

BICYCLISTS. This group—called the New Hampshire Wheelmen—posed on Pleasant Street on the occasion of their first meeting, September 18, 1882. The building on the right served as the offices of shipwrights Fernald and Pettigrew and still stands on the corner of Pleasant and State Streets, while the house on the left has been demolished.

CHARLES W. BREWSTER. This Davis Brothers *carte de visite* is of Charles W. Brewster, longtime publisher of the *Portsmouth Journal of Literature and Politics*. A series of his articles on old Portsmouth was collected in two volumes entitled *Rambles About Portsmouth*. Brewster's *Rambles* have been a prime source of local lore for historians. Small, wallet-sized photos used as calling cards, *cartes de visites* were popular in the late nineteenth century.